A NOTE TO PARENTS

This book requires cuddling during reading. Placing an arm around a child and simply saying "I love you, and Jesus loves you," can convey more than mountains of memorized Bible verses.

Help the child imagine what it might have been like in Jacob's day. Talk about times you've walked a long way to get to something or someone special. Talk about how it feels when you finally catch a glimpse of that person.

Children understand what it's like for adults not to want them around. This story reminds us that Jesus did not turn children away. Jesus welcomed them and hugged them tight, just as parents and grandparents hug children today.

— *Delia Halverson*

Delia Halverson is the consultant for *Family Time Bible Stories*. An interdenominational lecturer on religious education, she has written seven books, including *How Do Our Children Grow?*

Scripture sources: **Matthew 18:1-5, 19:16-30, Mark 10:13-16**

FAMILY TIME
BIBLE
STORIES

JESUS AND
THE CHILDREN

Retold by Mary Quattlebaum

Illustrated by Bill Farnsworth

ALEXANDRIA, VIRGINIA

Jacob and his mother and little Sarah left their home before sunrise.

Mother walked quickly, carrying a large bundle of wool for the market. "There will be a big crowd today," she said. "The great teacher Jesus is speaking. I hear he is very wise."

Sarah tugged Jacob's hand. "My feet hurt," she whimpered.

Jacob sighed. His feet hurt, too, and the long road was hot and dusty. Jacob had never heard of this teacher, Jesus. What wise words could he possibly say?

"I'll carry you," Jacob said, helping Sarah climb on his back.

Riding high, Sarah happily patted his head. "Go, good donkey," she said.

Finally they reached
the place where Jesus
would speak.

"Look," said Mother.
"Jesus is sitting under
that tree."

Jacob tried to look.
He looked to the right.
He looked to the left.
He looked up.

It was no use.
He saw nothing but legs.

"Jacob," said Mother,
clutching their bundle,
"why don't you take
Sarah closer to Jesus.
I'll watch you from here."

Gripping Sarah's hand, Jacob began to
push through the busy crowd. Around
them, grownups talked and called out.

Suddenly Jacob heard a voice. It was
low and kind.

Is that the voice of Jesus? Jacob
wondered. Inch by inch he crept closer
to the sound.

"Teacher," called one man. "What must I do to reach the kingdom of heaven?"

"You must follow God's rules," said the kind voice. "And you must love all other people as well."

"I do that," said the man happily. "I can enter your kingdom of heaven!"

The kind voice said, "And you must also give your money to the poor."

"Oh," said the man. Suddenly he did not sound so happy.

"Do not worry about money," the kind voice continued. "Do not think about riches on earth because you will have other riches in heaven."

"Oh," the man said again. Now he sounded very unhappy. Shaking his head, he disappeared from the crowd.

That man must want
money more than the
kingdom of heaven, Jacob
thought, continuing to
push through the crowd.
He knew he was close to
Jesus' tree.

Jacob looked to
the right. He looked to
the left.

He still saw nothing
but legs.

"I can't see," Sarah
declared. "Let's go closer."

Now Jacob could hear the questions from Jesus' followers, the disciples. "Teacher," said one disciple, "who is best in the kingdom of heaven?"

"I tell you," began the kind voice of Jesus, "the best are those who—"
"I still can't see!" shouted Sarah, tugging Jacob's hand. "I want to see Jesus!"

"Hush!" One disciple tried to shoo Sarah away. "What are you doing here, little girl?"

Sarah looked up, up at the tall disciple. "I want to see Jesus," she said.

"Girl, you are disturbing our teacher," grumbled another disciple. "Where are your parents?"

"I'm sorry," Jacob said, stepping between them. Embarrassed, he tried to lead Sarah away.

Then a hand reached through the crowd and took Jacob's hand. A kind voice spoke: "Please stay."

"Hello, Jesus," said Sarah, waving.

Jesus smiled before turning to the scolding disciples. "Quiet," he said, "and listen. You don't understand.

"I tell you," continued Jesus, "to enter the kingdom of heaven, you must become kind, innocent, and trusting. You must become ... exactly like children."

Jesus' smile grew wider. He called to the parents. "Bring your children to me. Do not stop them. For the kingdom of heaven is open to them and to others as trusting as them."

Jesus blessed every child in the crowd.

    After Sarah's blessing, Jacob started to take her back to their mother. Then he stopped, reached out, and touched Jesus' hand. "Thank you," he said shyly.

    Jesus looked at Jacob and Sarah. "You listen well, Jacob," he said ... and smiled.

TIME-LIFE KIDS®

Staff for FAMILY TIME BIBLE STORIES

Managing Editor:	Patricia Daniels
Art Director:	Susan K. White
Publishing Associate:	Marike van der Veen
Editorial Assistant:	Mary M. Saxton
Senior Copyeditor:	Colette Stockum
Production Manager:	Marlene Zack
Quality Assurance Manager:	Miriam Newton

First printing. Printed in U.S.A.   Published simultaneously in Canada.

Time Life Inc. is a wholly owned subsidiary of THE TIME INC. BOOK COMPANY.

TIME-LIFE is a trademark of Time Warner Inc. U.S.A.
School and library distribution by Time-Life Education,
P.O. Box 85026, Richmond, VA 23285-5026.
For subscription information, call 1-800-621-7026.

Library of Congress Cataloging-in-Publication Data

Quattlebaum, Mary.
Jesus and the children / retold by Mary Quattlebaum; illustrated by Bill Farnsworth.
p. cm. — (Family time Bible stories) Summary: Retells the classic Bible story of Jesus speaking to the children.
ISBN 0-7835-4628-9
1. Bible stories, English—N.T. Gospels. 2. Jesus Christ—Blessing of children—Juvenile literature. [1. Bible stories—N.T. 2. Jesus Christ—Blessing of children.]
I. Farnsworth, Bill, ill. II. Title. III. Series
BS2401.Q38 1995   95-25282
226'.09505— dc20   CIP
                                          AC